PORSCHE

GERMANY'S WONDER CAR

BY JAY SCHLEIFER

Crestwood House
New York

Maxwell Macmillan Canada
Toronto

Maxwell Macmillan International
New York   Oxford   Singapore   Sydney

To D. D.

Copyright © 1992 by Crestwood House, Macmillan Publishing Company

Crestwood House
Macmillan Publishing Company
866 Third Avenue
New York, NY 10022

Maxwell Macmillan Canada, Inc.
1200 Eglinton Avenue East
Suite 200
Don Mills, Ontario M3C 3N1

Macmillan Publishing Company is part of the Maxwell Communication
Group of Companies.

First Edition

Designed by R Studio T

Printed in the United States of America

10 9 8 7 6 5 4 3 2 1

Library of Congress Cataloging-in-Publication Data
Schleifer, Jay
Porsche / by Jay Schleifer.—1st ed.
p. cm.—(Cool classics)
Summary: Discusses one of the fastest and most exciting cars of all time and how it came
to be built by the man who also created the Volkswagen.
ISBN 0-89686-703-X
1. Porsche automobile—History—Juvenile literature. 2. Porsche, Ferdinand, 1875–1951—Juvenile
literature. [1. Porsche automobile—History. 2. Porsche, Ferdinand, 1875–1951. 3. Volkswagen
automobile—History.] I. Title. II. Series.
TL215.P75S36 1992
629.222'2—dc20   91-31534
                                                                    CIP
                                                                    AC

CONTENTS

Porsche has been producing some of the world's finest supercars for decades.

1 *AUTOBAHN* ADVENTURE

A little VW Beetle chugs along the *Autobahn,* Germany's version of a U.S. superhighway. The tiny car is loaded down with Mama, Papa, kids and dog. The family is off on a winter vacation in the Alps. They travel at night so they'll have more time to ski in the famous mountains.

There are no speed limits on these roads, but the Beetle is no threat to any world record. With its tiny sewing machine of an engine thrashing madly, it can barely break 70 mph. But if it could talk the little bug would proudly tell you it could run at that speed all day.

Suddenly a pair of distant headlights appears in the Bug's rearview mirror. In just seconds the powerful sports car catches up and is right on the VW's tail, flashing to pass. The car is a teardrop-shaped guided missile, pushing a wave of brilliant light from its driving lamps.

The Beetle driver isn't about to block the way of this super machine and he quickly pulls to the right. Then in a rush of wind the mystery machine blasts past, never to be seen again.

Just before the car disappears into the darkness, the boy in the backseat recognizes its shape. It's a twin-turbo, all-wheel-drive Porsche 959—one of the most exotic road cars in the world. And it's doing at least 180 mph!

The boy thinks about the Porsche. In a way he feels connected with this auto masterpiece. Both it and his dad's Beetle were invented by the same famous family of auto designers and engineers. Both VW and Porsche started with the same brilliant mind—that of Dr. Ferdinand Porsche.

This is the story of Dr. Porsche, the family he founded and the cars that proudly carry his name. It's a story that begins before the auto was invented, lasts through two world wars and for a time crosses paths with the evil world of Adolf Hitler. But in the end it drives to glory on the roads and racetracks of the world.

Come along for the ride!

 **THE PROFESSOR**

Think of the names Ford, Chevrolet and Chrysler. Have you ever wondered where these names come from?

The answer lies in auto history. All are the names of American auto pioneers. And all of them built a great car company.

In the same way Europe has its pioneers. Most have cars named after them. Among the greatest is Ferdinand Porsche.

Porsche was the engineer who created many designs we take for granted today. Whenever you see a Volkswagen Beetle chugging down the street, think of Dr. Porsche. He designed the Beetle. Whenever you hear of **torsion-bar suspensions** and **air-cooled** or rear-mounted engines, remember Dr. Porsche. He was among the first to make them work. And of course, remember him as the man behind the car that bears his name.

These achievements are even more amazing when we realize that when Porsche grew up, cars didn't exist. He was born in tiny Mattersdorf, Austria, in 1875. It was a time when horses and wagons still ruled the roads.

Porsche's father owned a metalsmithing business. He naturally expected his bright young son to take part in running it. But young Ferdinand had other ideas.

While some new Porsches have front engines, it's the rear-engined models that made the car famous.

While he loved mechanical things, he hated the gritty job of bending and filing metal parts. And he made it clear to his parents that he'd never spend his life in the metal business.

The Porsches did not fight their son's interests. Instead they sent him to the Imperial Technical School in Reichenberg so that he could decide what he wanted to do with his life.

There Porsche discovered a whole new world of exciting science. The big news of the day was electricity. But while other students studied it, Porsche looked for ways to put it to work. Before long he'd wired the family home. Most homes didn't even have lights, but the Porsches' had an electric doorbell! Ferdinand soon had an even better use for the new force. A local carriage maker had asked him if electricity could somehow propel his wagons.

Faced with this interesting question, Ferdinand Porsche raced to his drawing board. Soon he rolled out one of the most advanced electric-vehicle designs of that—or any other—time! Rather than using a large central motor, which most designers would have done, Porsche put small motors in each wheel. This allowed more power and cut down on weight. It was a brilliant idea!

Another inventor might have stopped there. But Porsche was not just any inventor. The battery that powered the motors was heavy and needed to be recharged often. So Porsche created a gasoline engine that made electricity for the motors. The battery wasn't needed anymore. This system of combining gasoline and electricity is called "hybrid power." Many of today's designers favor the system for future cars. Porsche had the idea almost 100 years ago!

As Porsche's skills grew, auto companies became aware of the brilliant young tinkerer from Mattersdorf. In 1905, when Ferdinand was just 30 years old, he became head engineer of one of Austria's largest vehicle factories.

But just as Porsche began to make his mark in auto design, World War I broke out. Carmakers were asked to turn their attention to making fighting machines.

Porsche had little interest in politics. His idea of victory was shaving weight off an engine or increasing its power. But he devoted all of his attention to the war effort. For the Austrian armed forces, he created advanced aircraft engines. He even used his gasoline-electric system for a "land train" to transport soldiers.

For this work Porsche received several medals—and a title. From then on, he would be Herr Professor Doktor Porsche.

3 THE PEOPLE'S CAR

When the war ended in 1918, times were hard in Austria and in neighboring Germany. After four years of fighting, these nations were exhausted. But at least Porsche could design automobiles again. He went to Germany to work for Daimler-Benz, the company that builds Mercedes-Benz cars. But the Professor soon decided that working for a single big company was not enough for him. He decided to open his own shop instead, near Stuttgart. That way he could design for anyone who wanted him. And maybe even someday he would create his own car.

One of Dr. Porsche's first customers, though, was not a car company. He was one of the most evil men that ever lived: Adolf Hitler. The year was 1934, and Hitler had come to power by promising to make Germany a great nation again after its defeat in World War I.

One of his promises was to make a car that any German could afford to own—a *Volkswagen,* which is German for "people's car." Hitler wanted it to be one of the most advanced cars in the world, yet sell for under a thousand dollars. Of course, Hitler didn't have the slightest idea how to build it. But he knew someone who did: Dr. Porsche. So he hired him to design and build the car.

To Porsche the project was more important than the person who had set him to work on it. He'd been playing with ideas for such a car for years. And soon there rolled from the Porsche shops an oddly shaped rear-engined machine that set the auto world on its ear. Hitler called the car the KdF-Wagen, or "Strength through Joy Car" (Naming autos was not his talent!). Today we know it as the Volkswagen Beetle.

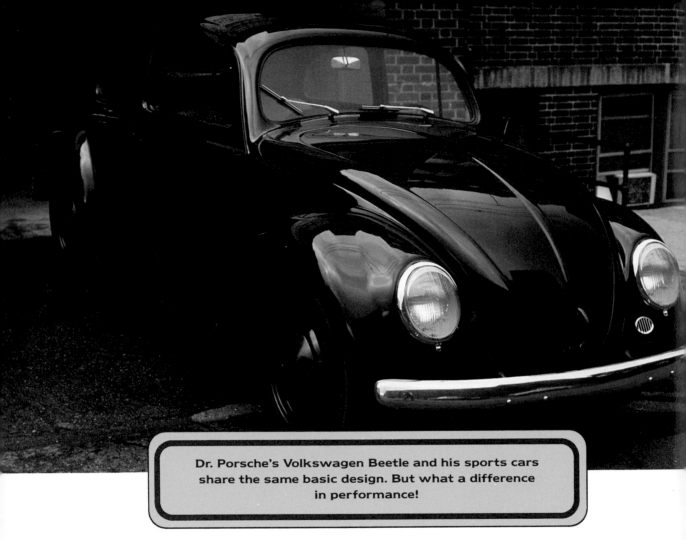

Dr. Porsche's Volkswagen Beetle and his sports cars share the same basic design. But what a difference in performance!

In time more than 16 million Beetles rolled off the assembly line, making it the most produced design ever. But the Beetle is important in this story for another reason. As part of the project, Porsche tried putting Beetle parts into a sports-car body. This was the beginning of Dr. Porsche's dream: his own sports car.

Hitler involved Dr. Porsche in other projects that later helped shape his sportster. One was to build a racing car for a German builder called Auto Union (now Audi). Hitler promised to back the car with many millions of dollars. He wanted a car that would show German greatness by blowing the competition away, and he didn't care what it cost.

As he did for the VW, Dr. Porsche gave the Auto Union racer a rear-mounted engine. But the VW was a family car and the racer was a fantastic V-16 design that pumped out 600 horsepower—incredible punch for the 1930s. When the German "silver bullets" showed up to race, few others stood a chance to win.

 ## THE TIGER AND THE MOUSE

As the Volkswagen project moved ahead, Dr. Porsche also helped plan a brand new plant to make it—a dream of a factory that would roll out a new VW every few seconds. It would be his own factory, though Hitler's money would back it. But just as Hitler smashed dreams everywhere, he destroyed those of Dr. Porsche. The dictator who had started World War II decided that the factory would build war machines instead of the Beetle.

As in World War I, Dr. Porsche turned his talents to the needs of his nation. Germany's magnificent Tiger tank was a Porsche design. So was the *Kübelwagen* ("bucket car"), the jeep version of the VW often seen in war movies.

Perhaps his most fantastic creation was a gigantic tank jokingly called the Mouse. It was a mouse that roared! Weighing 180 tons, the Mouse could not be stopped by enemy fire. But it was so heavy that it sank into soft ground, digging its own grave! It was one Porsche design that the doctor probably wanted to forget.

During the war the Porsche shops were large and lavish, with all the best equipment. But every U.S. bomber knew exactly where the shops were located. The German government had to find a safer place for them.

In 1943 Dr. Porsche and his factory were moved to Gmund, a tiny farming town in Austria. There one of the greatest design shops in the world had to operate from a run-down sawmill!

By the end of World War II little was left of the Porsche design company—or of Germany. The nation lay in ruins. What's more, the United States and its allies were not about to forgive anyone who had helped in the war effort. Porsche was not a government leader, but he was charged with war crimes and thrown into a dark, dank prison cell for nearly two years.

At the age of 70 this was more than the famous designer's health could take. He suffered a stroke and died a few years later. But before ill health had taken his life, the doctor was able to see two dreams come true: The VW plant was rebuilt, and his little "people's car" began covering German roads. And as part of that effort, the first Porsche sports car was born.

 THE FIRST PORSCHE

As it happened, Dr. Porsche didn't do much actual work on the sports car. The idea and the general design were his, but the doctor was too old and sick to do the work when the chance came. Fortunately there was another Porsche able to take over. This was Dr. Porsche's son, Ferdinand Jr., called "Ferry" since childhood.

Like his father, Ferry was a brilliant engineer, and he and his father often worked side by side. But they worked in different styles. Dr. Porsche liked to come up with the "big idea"—the break-through! Ferry took those ideas and slowly improved them. "Step by step to perfection!" was his motto. And putting that motto to work was a good way to develop a great sports car.

After World War II Hitler was no longer in power and Germany no longer had money to produce the Beetle. So the Porsche family was on its own. They wanted to move from the old sawmill in Gmund back to the main factory in Stuttgart. But they had no money either. And there wouldn't be any until the shattered German auto business was rebuilt. So Gmund would be home for a long time. But how would they feed and pay the Porsche workers?

The answer: Repair farm machinery! The lucky farmers around Gmund had their tractors cared for by some of the world's best auto engineers.

The workers also needed something creative to do. So finally Ferry and his talented crew laid down plans for the sports car the professor had long dreamed of—a car known as the Model 356.

The first drawings for the 356 looked like no other sports car in the world. The great roadsters of the time were Maserati and Alfa Romeo. These were swoopy machines with "mile-long" hoods and impressive radiator grilles that showed off their powerful in-line engines. Even small sportsters, like Britain's MG, tried to have a classic look. In contrast, the new Porsche design looked like a flattened VW Beetle—a sardine can on wheels. But there was a reason for the look: It was highly streamlined. And at that time streamlining was beginning to be popular.

As a Porsche design, there was only one place for the engine! The small, four-**cylinder** engine was mounted in the rear, behind the seats. Up front, where you would find most car engines, was a small trunk. In many ways it was the same setup used on the Beetle.

As for an impressive front, the car didn't even have a grille! There were just a couple of thin chrome stripes for decoration. That and the name, P-O-R-S-C-H-E, in big block letters. Ferdinand and his son had come up with many designs, but this was the first time the family's magic name actually appeared on a car.

13

To keep performance high and price low, the car featured lightness and simplicity. The body was made of **aluminum** that was beaten into shape by hand. The dashboard had only two dials—a speedometer and fuel gauge—that were placed on a bare metal panel. But the most important factor in keeping costs low was that almost all of the engine, and the complete braking and steering systems, came right off the Volkswagen Beetle. This meant that parts were easy to get.

Ferry Porsche's aims were clearly stated. "We wanted a car that was quick, light, agile and fun to drive," he said.

He got one. Although the new 356 had just 40 horsepower, it weighed a feathery 1,324 pounds. That combination, as testers soon found, gave the car a top speed of 90 mph—fast for the day. And like its cousin the VW, the 356 got 35 miles per gallon.

The 356 was the first design to carry the family name. It was light, simple and a blast to drive.

Tests were run all over Germany, from the *Autobahn* to the twisting mountain roads of the Alps. It seemed that there was nothing the new Porsche couldn't do. It stuck like glue on corners, as Porsches have ever since. And even with the low-powered VW engine, the car could take the steepest mountains in stride. Porsche engineers knew they had a winner in every way!

Even so, they followed Ferry's demands for constant improvement. A second model saw the engine placed behind the rear wheels instead of behind the seats. A sleek coupe body also joined the open roadster design of the original 356.

 **GAINING FAME**

With a superstar design in hand, the Porsche company now had a different problem: how to sell the car. A new company needed parts, service centers and dealers! And Porsche didn't have them.

Fortunately another new company did! The company was one that Hitler had created and Dr. Porsche had worked with: Volkswagen. Germany had picked up where Dr. Porsche had left off and continued building cars under the VW name. And it was growing even faster than Porsche.

Leaders of the two autobuilders met, and a deal was struck. In exchange for again helping Volkswagen design cars, Porsche got VW dealers to sell its cars. Now all Porsche had to do was build cars for the orders that came in. And the orders poured in as the car's fame spread.

Filling these orders was not as easy as it sounded. Porsches were mostly hand-built, and one important pair of those hands belonged to the man who beat the aluminum into shape for the

Early Porsches were mostly handbuilt. One man had the skill to beat the body panels into shape.

bodies. He was a skilled craftsman, but he sometimes drank too much. And when he was drinking, the plant couldn't produce anything.

Even when the body man was working steadily, the little sawmill at Gmund could only produce five cars a month. Porsche needed to return to its original factories near Stuttgart to make more.

In 1950 the company was finally able to make the move. Production skyrocketed, first to 60 and then to 80 cars a month. Porsche also switched to all-steel bodies. They no longer had to depend on the body man!

Things were going better, and Ferry decided that the time was right for another kind of move. He entered a little silver-gray Porsche in one of the world's great auto races—the 24-hour-event at Le Mans, France. Running against other small-engined cars, it won its class on the first try!

Not many people in the auto world noticed the Porsche victory. The headlines went to the Ferraris and other big-engined cars that took the overall title. But Porsche would bide its time and improve itself. Then, one day, the little cars from Germany would beat them too.

 PORSCHE COMES TO AMERICA

As the 1950s rolled on, Porsche became more and more famous across Europe. But in America the car was still unknown. That was about to change.

The man who made it happen was Max Hoffman, a legend in the foreign car business. From his little showroom in New York, Max introduced Americans to a whole new world of cars. He had an

The America model was longer and lower than the cars Porsche sold in Germany, but it was too expensive to be popular.

idea of what Americans wanted in a car. And he was seldom wrong.

In 1949 Hoffman brought the first two Volkswagens to America. This was one of his few mistakes. With the war still fresh in people's minds, nobody wanted to own "Hitler's car." So Hoffman decided to let someone else take on the business. This was another mistake! In time the VW became the number-one foreign car. More than half a million Beetles sold each year! Oh well, nobody's perfect!

One thing Max did do right was to import the Porsche. Ferry Porsche felt that a *few* cars a year might be sold in the United States. But Max insisted he could sell that many every week, especially to young people. After much discussion, Ferry agreed to build a special model for U.S. drivers called the Porsche America.

The Porsche America was a gorgeous roadster, but it was too expensive for Max's young buyers. So Max pushed for another design—a no-frills Porsche that anyone could afford. The car was the famous convertible Speedster. It was the bare-minimum Porsche. Even the windshield was cut down to save costs: the glass barely reached the driver's hairline. With the top up, you drove a Speedster with your chin between your shoulders! But you drove like the wind in this ultralight supercar of the highways! The Speedster became part of the Porsche legend.

Hoffman also played an important role in creating the black horse badge seen on all Porsche cars. Many people think this symbol is centuries old. But in fact Hoffman knew that an **emblem** would help the cars sell, so he simply drew it up on a dinner napkin. Part of the emblem was the symbol of the city of Stuttgart. Hoffman's feelings about an emblem were right on the money. People loved it.

One man who was drawn to the Porsche emblem was the famed actor James Dean. Dean was the "bad boy" of 1950s movies, the

Who says a sports car needs a fancy grille? The leather straps hold the hood down, even at high speeds!

"troubled teenager" who starred in *Rebel without a Cause*. Young people everywhere fell for his semisneer look and swept-back hair.

Everyone in Hollywood knew that Dean raced cars and that the cars he raced were Porsches. They also knew that he drove too fast for his own good.

James Dean was only 24 years old when he died on a California backroad—behind the wheel of a new Porsche racing car. The smashed car was later displayed at safety shows and a monument still stands at the site of the crash.

Dean is gone, but his memory lives on, even today. And Porsche is part of it.

8 SPYDERS AND CARRERAS

Porsche's long involvement with racing began with that first 356 model entered at Le Mans in 1951. From there it just grew and grew. The company realized from the start that every time a Porsche won a race, more of the road cars sold. For that reason many special models have been built just for the track.

In 1955 one of the most famous of those cars appeared. From the outside, it looked a lot like any 356 model. But a tiny badge on the rear told the true tale. The badge said "**Carrera**," the Spanish word for "race."

The Carrera featured a four-cam engine, the first one used by Porsche. **Cams** are rotating shafts that open and close an engine's valves. This lets in fuel and draws out exhaust. The faster these valves work, the faster the flow of gasoline. This creates power.

Most four-cylinder engines have just one cam, so one set of valves waits its turn while the cam operates the other set. Really hot four-cylinder engines have two cams. The Carrera had four. And just for good measure it also had twin sparkplugs to add more fire to the fuel.

You can guess the results. Combined with Porsche's usual lightweight body and stick-like-glue handling, Carreras were unbeatable against other cars in their class. They remain among the most valuable 356 models today and the name is still used on present Porsches.

Another special was the 550 **Spyder**, the car that took James Dean on his last ride. The Spyder (the name means open racer, not the eight-legged creature) was made for the racetrack. Road Porsches had their engines behind the rear wheels, but the Spyder had its engine in the middle of the car. This gave it better overall balance. A superlight aluminum body was then wrapped around the racing chassis.

There weren't any comfort features in the Spyder. The doors were like slots that you had to climb over. The windshield was nose high, and there was no top of any kind. Still, Porsche always had more orders than it could fill for the little beast. The Spyder remains among the rarest and most valuable of Porsches.

9 THE CLASSIC 911

By the late 1950s the Porsche sports car was a huge success. But the original 1947 design was quickly getting old. A totally new car would be needed in the very near future if the company was going to stay successful.

Talent runs in the Porsche family. There's as much of it as there is speed in the cars they build. Ferdinand was a genius. Ferry was the right man to take his father's ideas to fame. Now another Porsche enters the story. This is Ferry's son, Ferdinand Alexander Porsche III. Like his father, he has a nickname: Butzi.

When the need for a new car arose, Butzi was asked to head up the team that built it. He was told that the new car should be roomier *and* have improved performance. It should have more space *and* more speed. It also had to be totally new but still look like a Porsche. It was a tough challenge to meet.

Butzi was thrilled about the job. The first decision was a big one. The old four-cylinder engine had to go. The new car would be Porsche's first production six, but it would still have the same air-

The super-hot Carrera model added a four-cam engine to the 356's already high performance. Hold on to your seat belt!

cooled rear-engined design that began with the VW. Otherwise it just wouldn't be a Porsche!

With the layout in place Butzi headed for his drawing board to design the body. When he was done, the basic 356 lines were thinned and smoothed out. The sides were streamlined flat and airy windows were added for a bright interior. A grilleless front and vents at the rear left no doubt as to where the engine was. Butzi hoped that he had created a design that would last almost to the 21st century. And it has. Today's models look very similar. And they still look terrific!

What would they name the new car? Porsche uses a numbering system for all designs, and this was a big change from the old 356. So it got a big jump in model number. The new Porsche 901 was ready for display. Sports-car fans would wait no longer.

Hold it! Any Porsche lover knows that the classic Porsche is the *911*. So what happened to the 901?

When the car was announced, Porsche got a very angry letter from Peugeot, a French carmaker. "All our cars have three-number names with zero in the middle," said the giant Parisian company. "Look at these Peugeots: 404, 405, 505. And we don't want anyone to think your car is one of ours."

Porsche couldn't believe that anyone would confuse their elegant supercar with a line of French sedans often used as taxicabs. But 10 notches were quickly added to the new car to make the number 911, one of the most famous in auto history.

Just for good measure Porsche briefly added a 912 model, which featured the old four-cylinder engine in the new body. Few were produced, though, and the 911 soon motored on alone.

It motored with speed and grace. With six pounding pistons on board horsepower jumped to 130, even though the engine was just

two liters in size. Part of the reason for this were multiple cams, as on the Carrera. This allowed the engine to spin up to a spine-tingling 6,100 revs per minute (RPM). Zero to 60 came and went in just over eight seconds, with a top speed of 130.

These numbers were good, but there were other improvements as well. A new **suspension** system allowed for truly fine handling (the old car was a master in the turns, but drivers needed a firm hand to keep control). Also, Butzi's push for a roomier, airier cabin made this the first true luxury Porsche.

The all-new 911 Porsche came out in 1961. The same basic car is built today.

The Porsche 911 was a much better performance car than the 356. This turbo model features a "whale-tail" rear wing for better airflow.

With the 911 Porsche escaped its VW history to join cars like Ferrari and Jaguar. It had become one of the world's truly great cars.

Refined, improved and updated, the 911 series has continued into the 1990s as the most famous of all Porsches. Many say it is also the best. Porsche says it will go on as long as anyone still wants it. It may go on forever!

10 PORSCHE'S MISTAKE

Some say it looked like a doorstop. Others say it looked like a brick. Still others compared it to a shoebox with a handle. And hardly anyone believed that this ugly duckling came from Porsche. Yet that's exactly what the 914 model, built in the mid-1970s, was. How did such a thing happen?

The main reason was that the birth of the 911 also resulted in the end of the old 356 line. That left the company with just one rather high-priced car to sell. And after all it had spent on the 911, there was no money for anything else. Not until the phone rang, that is.

The caller was Volkswagen! The giant German company had decided it needed to spice up a dull line, and there was no better spice than a real sports car. The new car could use a VW engine, but VW lacked sports-car experience—and a real sports-car name. The idea of a "fast Volkswagen" was making people laugh.

"We'll bring the engine and the money," said VW. "You bring the engineering and the magic Porsche name."

The companies talked about it and then decided to do it. The car would be built by VW to keep costs down and sold through both sets of dealers, just like the first Porsche had been. It would be called the VW-Porsche in Europe, the Porsche 914 in the United States.

What an idea! But what should the car look like? Porsche had its ideas, of course, as did VW. To settle the issue, an outside designer was called in.

The first models looked good, but then the bickering began. When a key man at VW died and a new man took over, things started to go down hill. VW then tried to get more money from Porsche for the cars it sold, making the arguments even louder. And finally the United States passed new safety rules calling for fat

Some people compare the "ugly duckling" Porsche 914 to a brick with a basket handle. But it's still a fun car to drive.

bumpers and other changes. This caused problems with the design.

Through it all, the poor little 914 soldiered on. It really was a fine car, but owners of "true Porsches" sniffed and looked down on it. Owners of 914s were not even allowed to join some Porsche-owner clubs. They had to park outside.

When the 1970s ended, there was no more 914. But as sometimes happens, the car has now become a "cult" car, taken in like a poor orphan by a few drivers who out and out love it.

 RUNNING WITH THE BIG DOGS

In the 1960s Porsche made a big decision. They would make the 911 a car that could challenge the world's best—on the road and in the showroom. That meant Porsche also had to challenge Ferrari and the other big names where the rubber really hits the road— on the great racetracks. The time for class wins against small-engined cars was over. Porsche had to run with the big dogs or get out of the race.

Porsche's involvement in major league racing really began with a model called the 904. It featured the company's first use of a light **fiberglass** body, wrapped around the 911's six-cylinder engine (though early models used a Carrera four). The four and the six were still in the small-engined classes, but an eight-cylinder engine was built and fitted. Porsche was moving up—fast.

As model followed model in the 900 line, each was faster and more powerful than the one before. Engine size was going up, and Porsche was moving in other directions as well.

Porsches and racing go together. Here, two 944 models leave a little 914 in the dust.

Porsche racing cars were becoming real high-tech *Wunderkars* ("wonder cars"). They were built of unusual materials. They sprouted long tails and then wings, for better airflow at superhigh speeds. They became less and less like road cars and more and more like supersonic jets.

Until that time, the largest Porsche racing engines had been under three liters. But in 1968 race officials made a new rule. They would allow the fastest cars to have engines of up to five liters. The company made a key decision. They would add four more cylinders to their racing eight. Suddenly little Porsche was packing a 12-cylinder powerplant, just like Ferrari! The new engine pumped out more than 500 horsepower! The new car was the biggest, fastest Porsche of them all—the incredible Model 917.

"I fell in love with the 917," says Vic Elford, a top driver. "The car was unbelievably fast and it had a fearsome reputation. Other drivers just saw it in their mirrors and they'd pull over to the right and let us pass.... [One year at Le Mans] we were doing 230 mph in the rain. The following year we were doing 240!"

The 917's first year in racing was 1969, and it had its problems. But by 1970 the car was scoring its first wins. These weren't class wins but overall wins! Number one at the finish line!

The big prize, of course, was Le Mans, the killer 24-hour-race held in France each June. Four 917s were entered, and when the longest day in racing was over, it was Porsche that had won! What a shame the doctor hadn't lived to see it.

The 917 was just the first of the all-out racing Porsches. Later models, including the blindingly fast 962, added win after win.

By the mid-1980s Porsches were *expected* to win Le Mans and other top races each year. The big story was when someone else won. Porsche had done more than run with the big dogs. Porsche had *eaten* the big dogs.

⬡12 MOVING OUT IN FRONT

Ever since the first Porsche rolled from the sawmill in Gmund, the cars had had air-cooled rear engines.

Even when the new 911 was built, that didn't change. It was still a rear-engined, air-cooled design. It got to the point where if one thing in the auto world was sure, it was that Porsche would never build anything else. You could bet on it.

If you had you'd have lost. And you probably would have screamed as loud as "true Porsche fans" did when the first *front-engined,* **water-cooled** Porsche arrived in 1975. Its model number was the 924.

As with the other "non-Porsche" Porsche, the ugly duckling 914, the new car was born when Porsche and VW started talking to each other.

This time VW just wanted help in building a new car for their high-priced Audi division. The new car would use a water-cooled Audi four and be called an Audi. No Porsche version was planned.

But again there were management changes at VW, and the incoming bosses decided they didn't want the car. The new sportster was left all dressed up with no place to go.

Porsche thought it over. The company needed a new model, and here was a new model they had designed that nobody wanted. Ferry and his people took a deep breath and decided to make the car part of the family.

The first front-engined Porsche featured a single overhead-cam four-cylinder engine, with lots of high-tech goodies like **fuel injection**. It could also be bought with either a five-speed stick or a three-speed automatic transmission.

35

This is what the world knew as a Porsche until the front-engine 924 model came along.

The transmission location was unusual. Trannies are usually bolted directly to the engine, which would have placed the unit in the front of this car. But the 924's trannie was bolted to the rear end, in the *back* of the car, giving the car a front engine but a rear transmission, called a **transaxle**.

Porsche said it wanted to balance the heavy engine in front with the transaxle in back, so the weight distribution was more equal between front and rear. But some auto writers jokingly claimed to know better. They said Porsche was so used to rear-engined cars that they simply had to leave *something* back there!

The 924 was a neat little car, but with only 95 horsepower and a weight close to 2,700 pounds, it was no roadburner. (A more powerful turbo version came later.) Instead, another new Porsche —also front engined—was created to carry out the King of the Road role. This was the incredible Model 928.

The V-8 powered 928 model showed that Porsche could build a front-engine supercar. Its horsepower was 265 and its top speed was 150 mph!

This road warrior arrived in 1977 and showed that Porsche was dead serious about front-engined supercars. Designed to be called a Porsche from day one, it featured a massive 265-horsepower, 4.5-liter, water-cooled *V-8* engine, the company's first **vee** design. The most luxurious Porsche ever, the 928 also boasted the highest top speed ever in a Porsche built for the road—up to 150 mph.

The body design caused disagreements among auto writers though. Some felt it looked fast and muscular. Others called the shape a "giant gumdrop" and were bothered by the headlights, which lay flat on the hood. One writer said the lights looked like the eyes of a dead fish when lowered and those of a frog when raised. The car's $40,000 price shocked everyone. No Porsche had ever cost that much. Porsche had decided to challenge Ferrari openly, even in price!

The 928 proved a solid seller. And if you drove up to a restaurant in one, the doorman gave you the full "Yes sir!" treatment. Chances are he also parked it in the special spot out front. When you arrived in a 928, you *arrived!*

There's one more chapter to tell in the story of the front-engined cars. Many Porsche lovers had never really been satisfied with the performance of the little 924, and the factory knew it. The car simply needed a better engine than the Audi unit it was born with. But the cost of a totally new four was out of the question.

Besides, Porsche had a better idea. They just sliced the big 928 V-8 in half and had all the four anyone could ever need. Then the designers shoehorned this superfour into the 924 body and freshened up the styling with tough-looking bulges, as if to show that the car had grown muscles. The result was a new series, the 944. This best seller is the Porsche you're most likely to see on the streets today.

How do you make a model 944 four-cylinder engine? Get a 928 V-8 and a powerful buzz saw. Then cut the engine right in half!

13 SLANTNOSES AND WHALE TAILS

While all this engine news was happening in front, the rear-engined Porsches were making headlines too. Through all the front-engine experiments, Porsche kept improving the basic 911. An open model, the Targa, was introduced. Turbos were added, and special versions were tried out.

39

One was the famous "slantnose," a 911 turbo with a special sloping front. The inspiration for this car was the Porsche 935. This was a racer that packed over 600 horsepower and could pin a driver's ears back with a 0-to-60 mph time of just over three seconds. Top speed was better than 200 mph! The basic body of the 935 was that of the 911, but Porsche had fitted the sloping nose for better windflow on the racetrack.

With the 935 winning every race in sight, Porsche fans wanted at least the *look* of a 935 in their street cars. (The 935's "speed" parts themselves were totally illegal.)

Plastic body-part makers were happy to help. For about $25,000 they'd take your 911 and add a new front end. By the time

This is the actual 200-mph racing model 935 "slantnose." Many 911 owners wanted their cars to look like this.

Because of the demand, Porsche built a 911 with a 935 nose. It cost about $50,000 more than the standard 911.

the nose job was completed, your car looked just like the 935s that ran at Le Mans.

In time Porsche got tired of seeing all that money go into other pockets. The company then copied itself, putting out the "official" slantnose. For just $106,000 you could get the fake 935 look from the real source.

Another Porsche trademark is the "whale tail." It's a monster rear wing first used on the race cars and the 911 turbo. It serves a real purpose, making the air flow more smoothly off the car's sloped rear. But many Porsche fans love it just because it looks so outrageous. It had also been known to attract every traffic cop for miles around! But more and more 911 owners are adding it to their cars.

If you're a faithful moviegoer and TV watcher, you know that more and more Porsches have been showing up on the screen. One of the most famous was the convertible 911 turbo driven by Arnie Becker, one of the characters in the TV show "L.A. Law." Each week Arnie would tool around in his top-down turbo, spending a lot more time enjoying the California sun than he seemed to spend in court. Until the day Becker had to drive out to witness a house demolition, that is. What he witnessed instead was a bulldozer backing over his $90,000 sports car, flattening it like a tin can!

 **14** **TOMORROW'S PORSCHE**

Porsche has always been big on high tech. So when racing officials announced that they were starting a new racing class based on advanced design, the German engineers jumped at the chance. The series was called Group B, and just about anything was fine in design. Engineers could play around with turbos, four-wheel drive and other wild ideas.

Porsche's Group B car looked like a 911, with a familiar air-cooled six mounted at the rear. But from there on out, the car lived on the edge of automotive science.

Sporting two turbos, four cams, 24 valves and every electronic fad known, it pumped out 450 screaming horsepower from under three liters. All that power got to the ground through the most advanced four-wheel-drive setup ever. Zero-to-60 time was under

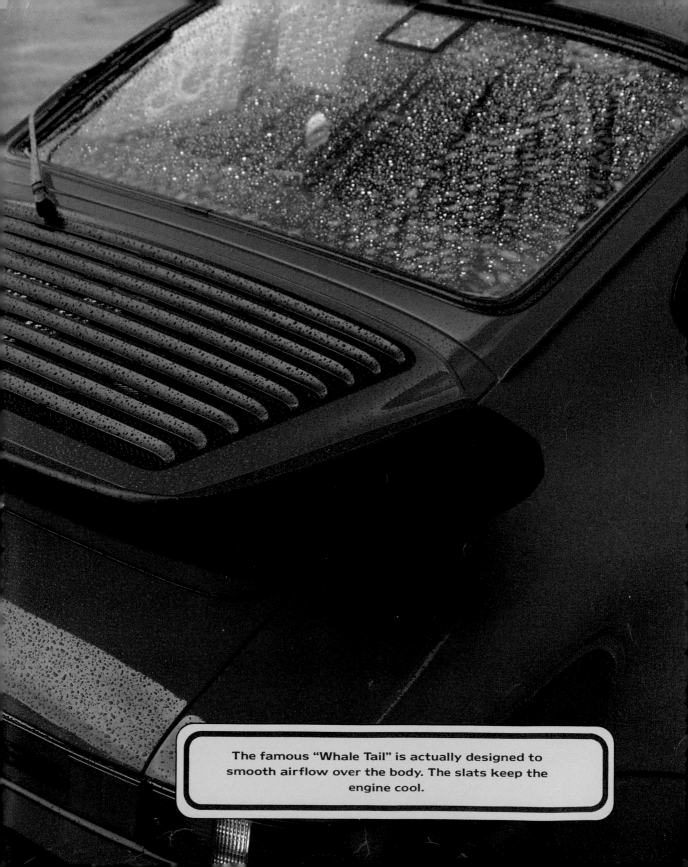

The famous "Whale Tail" is actually designed to smooth airflow over the body. The slats keep the engine cool.

four seconds and top speed was nearly 200 mph. Handling and braking were, said one car magazine, "hard to believe." Another called it a "Killer B."

Unfortunately the name turned out to be accurate. Almost as soon as Group B racing began, officials saw that the new cars were too fast to be safe. There were accidents and deaths, and the new class was canceled. A new Porsche was once again dressed up with no place to go. And going—as fast as possible—was this car's whole reason for being.

Porsche again decided to make the car part of the family, giving it the model number 959. There were about 200 of these cars built, and anyone who had the money could buy one. But we're talking money. The price of this ultimate Porsche was as high as $400,000!

Even so, Porsche had no problem finding enough rich car lovers and collectors to take all the 959s it could bolt together. And many now sit in well-heated garages and museums, never to run again. They're just too valuable to risk a smashup!

The 959 was valuable in another way. It taught Porsche some engineering lessons that are making their way into the company's other cars. The four-wheel-drive system, for example, has appeared on a 911 version called the Carrera 4.

Like other carmakers, Porsche doesn't like to talk about its future plans. But future plans definitely exist. The company recently spent millions on a new research and testing center in Weissach, Germany. This carrier is a kind of Porsche City for building new cars. There are rumors of a four-door "family" Porsche, which may be out by the time you read this. And going back to Dr. Porsche's original business, the engineering department still does design work for other car companies, though much of this work is secret. There's even a rumor that Porsche has done design work for a new

These days there is talk of four-door Porsches. But no matter what the factory builds, it will be a true performance car.

Russian car, though nothing like a 959 has been seen around the Kremlin yet.

Some things about the future are sure. Porsche will always build sports cars that are as advanced, fast, and exciting as possible.

One wonders how the doctor would feel about the way his dream has turned out. And about how much has happened since the first handbuilt Porsche sports car was hammered together in a sawmill.

We think he'd be proud of the Cool Classic that carries his name. And that he would call his Wunderkar just *wunderbar* (German for "wonderful")!

GLOSSARY/INDEX

air-cooled 6, 23, 26, 35, 42 A method of cooling an engine in which a large fan causes air to blow across the hot surfaces.

aluminum 14, 15, 23 A lightweight metal.

cam, or camshaft 22, 26, 42 A rotating shaft that pushes open the valves in an engine, causing them to admit the fuel-air mixture and allow exhaust gases to escape.

Carrera 22, 27, 32 Spanish word for "race" and the name for a series of high-performance Porsche cars.

chassis 23 The underparts of a car.

cylinder 13, 22, 23, 26, 32,34 The empty chamber in which gas is exploded in an engine; the force of the explosion then moves the piston, which in turn eventually turns the wheels of the car.

emblem 20 The visual symbol of a car company, usually shown in a badge on the car; the Porsche symbol is a black horse on a shield.

fiberglass 32 A plasticlike material used in car bodies, as well as crash helmets, skis and other goods; fiberglass is light and strong, is easy to work and will not rust.

fuel-injection 35 A system that actively pumps the fuel-air mixture into an engine rather than having it drift in through a carburetor.

Spyder 22 European term for an open sports car.

suspension 27 The system that mounts the wheels to a car chassis and allows them to flex up and down with bumps in the road.

torsion-bar suspension 6 A system in which the force of a bump is absorbed in the twisting of springy metal bars instead of in coil springs; torsion-bar systems occupy less room under the car and may provide better control.

transaxle 36　A chassis part combining the transmission and final drive system in one unit, rather than the usual two.

vee-engine layout 38　Arrangement of cylinders in a "V" shape within the engine; most often set up as a V-6 or V-8, though there have been V-4s, V-12s and V-16s; Dr. Porsche designed a V-16 racer in the 1930s.

water-cooling 35, 38　A system of piping liquid around hot engine parts to remove the heat; the liquid is then pumped through a radiator, which allows the heat to escape into the air.